WHOLE-FOOD PLANT BASED COOKBOOK

© Copyright 2022 Maggie A. White

Whole-Food Plant Based Cookbook

© Copyright 2022 All rights reserved.

Written by Maggie A. White

Limited Liability

Please note that the content of this book is based on personal experience and various information sources, and it is only for personal use.

Please note the information contained within this document is for educational and entertainment purposes only and no warranties of any kind are declared or implied.

Readers acknowledge that the author is not engaged in providing medical, dietary, nutritional or professional advice, or physical training. Please consult a doctor, nutritionist or dietician, before attempting any techniques outlined in this book.

Nothing in this book is intended to replace common sense or medical consultation or professional advice and is meant only to inform.

Your particular circumstances may not be suited to the example illustrated in this book; in fact, they likely will not be. You should use the information in this book at your own risk. The reader is responsible for his or her actions.

The information provided herein is stated to be truthful and consistent, in that any liability, in terms of inattention or otherwise, by any usage or abuse of any policies, processes, or directions contained within is the solitary and utter responsibility of the recipient reader.

By reading this book, the reader agrees that under no circumstances is the author responsible for any losses, direct or indirect, which are incurred as a result of the use of the information contained within this document, including, but not limited to, errors, omissions, or inaccuracies.

Table of contents

INTRODUCTION

Every year we are flooded with new diets or diets that come back into fashion, and sometimes it is difficult to judge whether following them is a good idea.

So why choose to start a nutritional journey based on plant foods in their most whole and natural form possible?

There are many answers, and you will discover them as you read the various chapters that follow.

And for those who are inclined to think that we are talking about a very restrictive and unvaried diet, I am sure they will reconsider their thinking by experimenting with the many recipes offered in this book and on the web.

Basically, the star foods of a WFPB diet are a wide variety of fruits and vegetables, whole grains and legumes, nuts and seeds, herbs and spices.

It does not include the consumption of animal protein (meat, fish, milk and eggs) or foods processed by industry.

The reason for this exclusion comes from the outcome of numerous scientific studies published in the most prestigious international journals such as "Science" that consider Foods rich in animal proteins and sugars pro-inflammatory. Furthermore their inflammatory power increases when it comes to foods processed by the food industry.

Thus, we can say that even science recommends that we reduce these foods because this seems to be the most effective way to regain our well-being.

But what are the main benefits on our well-being that a WFPB diet can generate?

Here are the four main ones:

Weight Control

Regarding weight loss, the principle of calorie deficit cannot be missing for this type of diet either: no deficit no pounds lost. Although this is not the motto of any diet, it is the "hidden" principle behind all diet plans for weight loss.

A plant-based diet was not born as a weight-loss diet, but in any case, following it, weight loss is the natural consequence because the foods it includes are low in calories and satiating as they are rich in water and dietary fiber,

The accumulation of body fat, particularly that concentrated in the abdomen, is an early symptom of the development of other diseases such as diabetes, autoimmune diseases, and cancer diseases.

Therefore, it is important not to underestimate this first clue that the body gives us and act immediately to make the metabolic system work well.

For this purpose, a plant-based diet helps us because:

- contains a lot of fiber that has a satiating and satisfying effect, so it will take some time before you feel hungry again after eating

-it contains little saturated fats

Thus, this diet shows that it is not necessary to count calories or limit the amount of food, but it is more useful to increase the quality of food.

Increased Energy

People who follow a plant-based diet rest better, have more energy and are able to improve their sports performance.

In fact, athletes who follow this diet benefit from the improved blood circulation and oxygenation that a plant-based diet generates in the body.

Health and Longevity

In general, a WFPB diet leads to a reduction of inflammation levels in the body and strengthens the immune system.

In this way alone, several chronic diseases can be prevented, stopped or cured.

These include diseases of the heart, respiratory system, diabetes, cancer, and cognitive diseases.

Safeguarding the Planet and Animals

Compared to animal breeding, plant-based farming generally has much less impact on the environment.

Preferring a plant-based diet can prevent the suffering of animals on intensive farms and the depletion of the oceans.

It is also an important step in preventing other pandemics related to animal consumption and trade.

CHAPTER 1

Comparing Various Plant-Based Diets for a More Informed Choice

What differentiates the WFPB diet from the vegetarian, vegan diet?

Simple: a Wole food diet emphasizes primarily health, while vegetarian and vegan diets, are associated primarily with the ethical idea of:

not wanting to kill and exploit animals

caring for our planet.

To make matters more complicated are then the "Plant Based" diets. These, unlike the WFPB diets, are primarily plant-based, but do not necessarily place restrictions on refined and processed foods (packaged foods, fast foods, white sugar, etc.).

Having said that, if we compare all these diets can we find more differences or more similarities?

Here is a chart that clarifies ideas on this topic:

	VEGETARIAN DIET	VEGAN DIET	PLANT BASED DIET	WHOLE FOOD PLANT BASED DIET
Meat and fish	NO	NO	NO	NO
Dairy products and eggs	YES	NO	NO	NO
Processed and refined food	YES	YES	YES	NO
Vegetable oils	YES	YES	YES	LOW CONSUMPTION
fruits, vegetables grains, legumes, seeds, nuts	YES	YES	YES	YES

As the chart also shows us, compared to the guideline of all plant-based diets, the WFPB is the only diet that excludes processed and refined foods.

But what is meant by unprocessed foods?

It is not always crystal clear which foods should be considered truly whole and unprocessed. To clear this doubt we are helped by Dr. M. Greger, who provides an interesting key to learning how to distinguish all natural, whole foods from all others

"Unprocessed foods are all those to which nothing harmful has been added and nothing healthy has been taken away."

According to this principle, foods from which the very healthful fiber, for example, has been taken away are to be avoided.

The following belong to this category: white sugar, white flour, white rice, as well as pearl barley and filtered fruit juices.

On the contrary, foods to which harmful elements have been added are:

- pre-packaged foods such as ready-made sauces, snacks, ready meals and desserts,
- junk food (fast food), which generally contains additives such as refined sugar, preserved foods, low-quality fats, dyes and flavorings.

It is important, in order to achieve higher levels of awareness about what we eat, to learn to check the food labels so that we can recognize each ingredient and recognize the quality of what we buy.

But then why are some foods that have undergone processing allowed in a WFPB?

We are talking about foods such as tofu, tempeh, bitter cocoa, miso, flaked yeast, and tomato pulp.

Simple: it is true that they are processed, but…

they have lost no nutritional value and need no harmful additions!

First Steps Toward a WFPB Diet and How to Make it Sustainable

If yours is currently an "omnivorous" diet, I recommend approaching the WFPB diet in small steps, including more and more vegetables in your diet.

Each time you choose a vegetable food instead of an animal food, and each time you choose, for example, a homemade bean soup instead of a prepackaged one, consider it as one more step toward your well-being.

I recommend that you start by gradually increasing the amount of vegetables on your plate, then begin to include one whole meal a week of only plant foods, then try to include one meal a day, and so on.

To take full advantage of the benefits of this diet, it is necessary to make it *SUSTAINABLE* over time.

If you set too many limits right away, you risk abandoning everything and easily slipping back into previous "unhealthy" eating habits.

There are people who, despite knowing the benefits of a whole-food plant-based diet, for various reasons fail to follow it radically.

It certainly depends on personality, on how determined one is to achieve a goal despite the difficulties we all initially encounter when changing our habits.

Of course, the society does not help us, because it is difficult to find restaurants aligned with the principles of a WFPB diet and it is difficult to have friends and family members who follow this diet.

Don't forget, however:

the sooner you start giving your body the best nutrition, the sooner you can notice the many positive changes that will involve your appearance, fitness, vitality levels, and overall health!

In addition:

these changes will be encouraging and will help you move on before you even get used to them!

Personally, I don't judge a person by what they eat and I don't like to be a "purist" at all costs.

I made a choice to regain my health, which, after the age of 40, I was gradually losing.

I am grateful to this diet because I achieved my goal and today I feel like a new person, stronger, more aware and proud of my body.

I discovered through this diet that the body has extraordinary regenerative and self-healing powers. So why not activate them?

I was so exasperated with jumping from one diet to another without getting satisfactory results that when I discovered this diet, I jumped into it 100% in only a few days and have been following it for over a year with great satisfaction.

But remember that your first goal is to succeed in a long-term healthy eating plan, because only then you will get satisfactory results. So if your best compromise is to indulge in the occasional gluttony, do it without feeling guilty. I am convinced that it is not occasional gluttony that makes the difference when eating habits are healthy.

This is why the book is titled WFPB for Everyone, because everyone can approach a healthy eating regimen according to their own desires and expectations, without having to **EVER** feel imprisoned in a diet regime.

Which Foods to Choose and to What Extent

There are many varieties to discover in the kingdom of plant and whole foods. When approaching this way of eating, it can be helpful to have a guide to make sure you are getting all the nutrients you need in a balanced way.

Fortunately, there is a list of the "Magnificent Twelve Foods," created by Dr. M. Greger, which includes all the foods that are recommended to be consumed daily and also an idea of the minimum amounts.

You can see in the table below what the list includes. (The number of ticks after the food indicates the number of daily servings to incorporate).

The Magnificent 12	Recommended Daily Portions
Legumes	3 portions
Whole grains	3 potions
Berries	1 portion
Other fruits	3 portions
Cruciferous	1 portion
Green leaf	2 portions
Other vegetables	2 portions
Linseed	1 portion
Dried fruits	1 portion
Herbs and spices	1 portion
Beverages	5 portions
Exercise	30 minutes a day
Vitamin B12	2,5 mcg day

A small disquisition about introducing legumes into one's diet.

In fact, for those who are not used to eating legumes, I recommend a soft approach with this food group. In this case, it is best to include a minimal amount to begin with and then increase day by day.

This is because the intestinal flora needs time to increase the bacteria that can help us digest legumes well.

Any feelings of bloating and meteorism, even for weeks, are usually only temporary, however.

Finally, in the transition phase it is possible to feel the effects of detoxifying the body in the form of headaches or fatigue. But this usually passes within a few days, and thereafter the positive effects take over.

CHAPTER 2

The Origins of Plant-Based Diets

Veganism

Many are led to believe that veganism is a fairly knew reality, but in fact veganism started in the distant 1847 in Ramsgate (England), with the founding of the Vegetarian Society, the oldest vegetarian organization in the world. In the early twenties, this association found itself divided into two factions: associates who preferred a vegetarian diet and those who refused the consumption of dairy products and other derivatives of animal origin.

Hence the Vegan Society and the term Vegan, which is the result of some of the first three letters with the last two of the word "Vegetarian," were born.

By 1945, "The Vegan" magazine already had 500 subscribers, and the vegan thought spread rapidly, succeeding in spreading a new awareness related not only to food but also to various issues related to the environment, respect for animals, and social coexistence.

A true cultural revolution, a change of course in the way we approach everything around us, a true philosophy that in a short time managed to involve also the fields of natural medicine, agriculture and food studies.

In 1970 this movement also aroused the interest of "official" medicine, so much so that it encouraged the start of new research, particularly in the United States, which led to the demonization of diets based on animal fats and proteins, defining them as harmful to health.

In 2010, a significant percentage of the world's population adopted the vegan philosophy, and this was also aided by increased access to previously hard-to-find food resources.

People who choose to be vegan do so not only for moral reasons, but also because they are convinced that only a certain type of vegan diet can have the effect of not making people sick and even healing their illnesses if they were already sick.

Whole-Food Plant Based

The term WFPB was introduced by Dr. T. Campbell around 1980 in the context of cancer studies.

Campbell conducted a huge epidemiological study in China and wanted to publicize the results by writing numerous books that could spread his findings as widely as possible to the public.

In the early 1980s, he conducted extensive studies on the relationship between diet-nutrition-cancer.

His research showed that a diet based mainly on the consumption of low-fat, high-fiber foods can both prevent the onset of cancer and, in people already ill, significantly slow the development of the disease.

The foods with these important healing powers to which the doctor referred were mainly vegetables, fruits, and whole grains.

Dr. Cambpell, however, could not call this diet either "vegetarian" or "vegan."

In fact, in examining these two types of diets, he had noticed that the vegan one consumes too many foods of animal origin (such as dairy products and fish) and included too much fat, while the vegan one tends to consume too many processed foods and too much fat.

So, wanting to name his diet to make it recognizable to the public, he identified two words that could best describe it **WHOLE** and **PLANT**. Thus the **WHOLE FOOD PLANT BASED** diet was born, which abbreviated became the **WFPB** diet.

CHAPTER 3

Anti-inflammatory diet + Alkaline diet = Stronger immune system

WFPB is an anti-inflammatory diet

According to the latest evolutionary theories, inflammation appears to be one of the most effective ways in which the body responds to various external and internal stimulus

Without a good inflammatory response, not even a simple wound could heal.

Inflammation, like stress, must be an emergency response, as necessary in the short term as it is deleterious when permanently active.

When it becomes a permanent, systemic state, inflammation itself becomes the cause of many modern diseases such as cardiovascular disease, hypertension, diabetes, dementia, obesity, cancers, autoimmune diseases, etc.

As written in the famous journal "Science," having identified inflammation as the pathophysiological mechanism that triggers all chronic diseases is one of the most important insights medicine has had in the past two decades.

Most of the population suffers from latent inflammation that remains apparently harmless.

A diet based on foods containing lactose, gluten, omega-6 (such as sunflower oil and foods processed by the food industry in general) and sugar triggers the onset of latent inflammation that is bound to become chronic.

Obesity itself causes inflammation, generating a vicious phenomenon whereby inflammation makes weight loss more difficult.

Most scientific studies today place the plant-based diet first as the diet with the highest anti-inflammatory power, due to its balanced fiber and healthy fat content.

A WFPB diet has an even more intense anti-inflammatory effect than other plant-based diets because it is the "cleanest."

WFPB is an Alkalinizing Diet

A WFPB diet manages to keep the acid-base ratio of our body in excellent balance. That is the goal of all alkaline diets. In fact, only in this way will our gut microbiota be in balance and our gut stay healthy and efficient.

It all depends on the PH measurement that allows us to keep track of our body's acid-base balance by expressing it through a precise value.

PH is measured on a scale ranging from 1 to 14 (we speak of acidic PH for values below 7 and alkaline PH for values above 7). To distinguish acidic from alkaline foods, it is necessary to measure their PH level after digestion. Assuming that the blood PH level is slightly acidic, to maintain our acid-base balance at an optimal level, it is advisable to favor alkaline foods.

According to what principles can foods be considered acid-based or alkaline-based?

To determine the basic acidity level of foods, the ash that remains after digestion of the food is analyzed.

It is important to note that there are foods that are classified as acid base but that actually, after a series of chemical reactions that activate digestion, are transformed into alkaline base. This is what normally happens in healthy individuals. The best known indicator for measuring the PH level of a food is the Potential Renal Acid Load, also known as the PRAL index. This index divides foods into two categories:

- foods with PRAL + have an acidifying effect (such as dairy products, fish, eggs, meat and fish).
- foods with PRAL - are alkalizing (fruits and vegetables).

WFPB Diet Strengthens the Immune System

The immune system is the body's first defense line, the rapid response mechanism against the attack of pathogens. Having weak immune defenses, therefore, means being more exposed to disease and infection.

This defense mechanism is most influenced by the gut: consider that 80 percent of the cells responsible for the functioning of the immune system are located in the gut.

In its interior, the gut is populated by entire colonies of microorganisms that form the microbiota. A balanced microbiota ensures us against the dangerous and latent general inflammatory state that puts us at greater risk of getting sick.

An alkaline and anti-inflammatory diet, such as a plant-based diet, affects the overall efficiency of our immune system.

What micronutrients must the food we eat contain to keep the immune system efficient?

- Fatty acids: these are the backbone of the cell, that is, its outer layer. Viruses need a host cell to enter and multiply. For this reason, a diet rich in healthy fatty acids-such as those in avocados, nuts, seeds, olive helps strengthen the outer layer of cells, making it more difficult for viruses to enter.
- Antioxidants are molecules that help the body defend itself against the attack of harmful agents and the state of oxidative stress.

- **The most important antioxidants are:**

Glutathione: produced by our bodies, is found in some vegetables such as avocados, spinach, peaches, and apples. There are also foods that can stimulate the production of glutathione that include those rich in selenium such as garlic, onions, fruits, and red vegetables.

Vitamin C: Contained in a high concentration in all green vegetables, berries, and citrus fruits; it is advisable to intake this vitamin directly from fresh foods rather than from supplements because it has greater bioavailability.

Vitamin D: A deficiency of this vitamin is directly linked to an inefficient immune system; recent surveys have found vitamin D deficiency in more than 70 percent of the world's population. Plant foods and particularly mushrooms are rich in it.

B-Carotene (precursor to vitamin A): found mainly in carrots, pumpkin, parsley, ripe tomatoes, broccoli, and kale."

Other micronutrients useful for keeping the immune system efficient and ready to react to external "aggressions," are:

Selenium, Zinc and Copper, important metals for their antioxidant activity, found in legumes, mushrooms, and, almonds.

Probiotics and prebiotics contained in all fruit and vegetables keep the microbiota healthy as they are rich in fiber.

As you may have noticed, all these elements are precisely what make up the alkaline and anti-inflammatory diet.

CHAPTER 4

How to Make WFPB an Even More Empowering Diet

1. Frequently consume these foods classified as "superfoods"

Avocado:

A true concentration of healthy nutrients. It is rich in potassium and magnesium, mineral salts that intervene in all cellular exchanges: rich in fiber and fatty acids. The latter are easily used by our body to produce energy, avoiding insulin peaks that lead to the accumulation of body fat. Recent studies have shown how useful avocado is to prevent cancer, especially stomach and pancreatic cancer, to combat osteoporosis and to reduce the symptoms of depression.

Blueberries and red fruits:

Like all very colorful vegetables, these fruits are very rich in antioxidants that slow down cellular aging; they also have a detoxifying and anti-inflammatory function and help lower blood sugar levels; they promote the increase of healthy HDL cholesterol thus strengthening the entire cardiovascular system. Although low in sugar, they are full of flavor that should not be missing in smoothies, salads….

Cumin:

A spice with a very intense aroma that comes from a herbaceous plant from which its seeds are extracted and dried; rich in calcium, magnesium, phosphorus, vitamin A, vitamin E; great for strengthening the immune system and helps keep pathogenic viruses away.

Cinnamon:

Known all over the world for more than 2000 years; rich in phenols that slow down the putrefaction of certain foods; it is known for its aphrodisiac effect and for its ability to enhance flavors in the kitchen; regulates cholesterol levels, facilitates digestion, reduces blood glucose levels, enhances energy and it also has beneficial effects on the mood.

Cabbage and broccoli:

Crucifers are very resistant to cold climates and are very rich in antioxidants such as vitamin K, vitamin A, vitamin E, magnesium, omega-3 fiber, iron, and potassium. A hundred grams of broccoli contain 150% of our average daily requirement of vitamin C; medical literature recognizes these vegetables as having strong anticarcinogenic power; they prevent diseases such as diabetes, and osteoporosis, fortify the immune system and promote weight loss because they have the ability to satiate. They are rich in fiber, which allows food to move faster through the intestinal tract and thus assimilate less simple sugars. They are best consumed raw or blanched in a pan.

Coconut oil:

Extracted from the fruit. Rich in MCT medium-chain triglycerides, which are more easily used by our body to produce energy than animal fats defined as long-chain; for this reason, when coconut is eaten, its fats are immediately oxidized by the liver, providing energy immediately; it is therefore very suitable for those who practice sports, but it is also suitable for those who want to lose weight because on the one hand it prevents the accumulation of body fat and on the other hand it has strong satiating properties.

It also has a strong antibacterial, viral and fungal capacity due to the lauric acid it contains.

Turmeric:

It is an antioxidant spice with strong anti-free radical and anticancer potencies, recognized as very important by holistic and Ayurvedic medicine. Its active ingredient, curcumin, has anti-inflammatory effects, which is why it is used to treat arthritis, inflammation, osteoarthritis, and joint pain. An additional benefit of turmeric is that it protects the immune system.

Chocolate:

It should have a high percentage of cocoa, so at least 80 percent, and should be raw if possible.

It is good to consume no more than 30 grams per day.

Chocolate is referred to as the "food of the gods."

Rich in:

- magnesium
- antioxidants
- tryptophan that is an essential amino acid able to relax the nervous system and increase the quality of your sleep
- polyphenols that improves brain functioning and slows down cognitive decay.

- flavonoids that protect the internal wall of blood vessels, regulates blood pressure and cholesterol.

In the recipe section, you will find some tasty chocolate desserts!

2. If you have any deficiencies, make use of dietary supplements

Vitamin B-12

Vitamin B-12 is essential for healthy blood and neurological cells and for DNA production.

In general, people who follow vegan or vegetarian dietary plans, as well as the elderly, are at risk of developing B-12 deficiency.

Symptoms of B-12 deficiency include fatigue, depression, tingling in the hands and feet, and anemia.

Omega-3 Essential Fatty Acids

Fundamentally, omega-3 essential fatty acids are composed of the various components of cell membranes. They aid the following areas:

- brain functioning and visual health energy
- maintaining good heart health and a good cardio circulatory system

Vitamin C or Ascorbic Acid

Although a plant-based diet is rich in foods that contain vitamins, it can still be important to supplement this vitamin because today's growing soils are less fertile than those of the past, and as a result fruits may not have the high concentrations of vitamin C that they once did.

We are also talking about a vitamin that is easily degraded by heat, so we may not always be able to assimilate it in the right amounts.

It is one of the most important vitamins because it is involved in many metabolic and enzymatic processes:

- It strengthens the immune defenses, increasing the ability of immune cells to produce antibodies; it increases the body's ability to better resist all diseases.

- It has a detoxifying effect on the body (toxins from smoking or pollution).

- It protects and repairs tissues by acting on collagen production; the latter safeguards the functioning of cartilage, bones, skin, capillaries and gums.

- It is an antioxidant because it counteracts the negative effects of free radicals, i.e., those molecules that push our bodies toward premature aging.

- It is useful in cases of anemia because it improves the assimilation of iron, an important mineral for the production of red blood cells.

- It helps reduce stress by promoting the synthesis of molecules that maintain stable nerve impulse transmission; it also regulates the synthesis of the stress hormone.

Vitamin D

Our bodies are only able to synthesize vitamin D when we expose ourselves to the sun.

For those who rarely expose themselves to the sun or only at certain times of the year, it may be helpful to supplement this vitamin in their diet.

This vitamin is very important:

- For the proper mineralization of bones and teeth because it helps maintain an optimal level of calcium in the blood

- To help keep our kidneys, arteries and body tissues healthy

- To strengthen the system against infections and immune viruses

- To maintain the functionality of the heart and cardiovascular system.

3. Drink a lot of water

Drinking plenty of water a day is important, because water is essential for a healthy and functional body; furthermore, water helps the absorption of nutrients.

CHAPTER 5

Whole Food Plant Based and Sport

Sport activity doesn't just help you lose weight and sculpt your body. It's first and foremost a choice to keep us healthy.

In order to carry out proper sports activities, it is necessary to know how to feed our bodies with "clean" foods that provide us with the energy we need and promote the body's recovery after playing sports.

Many famous athletes, such as Carl Lewis, have been shown to be able to achieve high-level sports performance by following a plant-based diet.

Those who follow a vegetable-based diet perform well in sports and, more importantly, recover very quickly after sports activity.

What contributes to the feeling of fatigue when playing sports is the lactic acid that the body produces.

By following a vegetable-based diet, the body produces less lactic acid, and the lactic acid produced by the body under stress is "buffered" and disposed of more quickly because the tissues are already alkaline.

For those who practice sports, it is best to choose high-protein plant foods, such as legumes. The most protein-rich legumes are:

- soybeans
- broad beans

- lupins

Even among cereals, it is best to choose those with a higher protein content:

- oats

- amaranth

- spelt

- quinoa

- buckwheat

Finally, oilseeds and dried fruits are a real concentration of proteins: among the most protein-rich ones there are: pumpkin seeds,

- linseeds

- sesame seeds

- pine nuts

- almonds

The most famous "doping" for athletes who eat vegetables is spirulina, because it is rich in protein and iron.

There are, therefore, some tricks to increase sports performance-just get to know them!

High-Protein WFPB Weekly Menu Ideal for Athletes – Easy, Heathy and Tasty

These recipes are suitable for all phases of the life cycle, including pregnancy, breastfeeding, early and late childhood, adolescence, adulthood, for the elderly, and athletes."

There is adequate protein in the menu I have prepared for those who exercise daily and want to follow a proper diet, but it is not suitable for competitive athletes who need a targeted and specific food plan based on their sport activities.

The nutritional values refer to an average serving of about 200 grams.

MONDAY

Breakfast

Blueberry Smoothie

Serve: 1

Ingredients:

- 200 gr soy yogurt
- 100 gr of fresh blueberries
- 1 tablespoon of chia seeds
- dark chocolate chips to taste

Preparation:

Blend the soy yogurt with the chia seeds and blueberries, keeping some aside for decoration. Serve in a small cup and add dark chocolate chips to taste.

Notes:

Soy yogurt provides quality plant protein. Blueberries are rich in anthocyanins, which plays an antioxidant role, as well as promoting the proper functioning of microcirculation. Chia seeds, an excellent alternative to flax seeds, are used to provide the right amount of omega 3.

Nutrition	Carbohydrates (g)	Protein (g)	Lipids (g)	Energy (Kcal)
	39	11,9	5,6	232

Lunch

<u>Chickpea Pasta Flour with Creamed Peppers</u>

Serve: 1

Ingredients:

- 100 g chickpea pasta
- half a bell pepper
- 2 tbsp soy milk
- parsley to taste

Preparation:

Blanch the bell pepper for a few minutes to soften it and to make it easier to remove the skin.

Blend the bell pepper with the soy milk and a pinch of salt to create a smooth, flavorful cream.

Separately cook the pasta for as long as needed and toss it with the creamy sauce.

Add a sprinkle of parsley and serve.

Notes:

Chickpeas are a good source of vegetable protein, rich in iron that we also find in the form of pasta. Bell pepper is a typical summer vegetable which is suitable for various preparations. It is rich in vitamin C and it should not be overcooked to avoid losing this vitamin in the cooking water. Parsley completes this recipe giving it color and flavor, providing vitamins and antioxidants with an anti-cancer action.

Nutrition	Carbohydrates (g)	Protein (g)	Lipids (g)	Energy (Kcal)
	52,1	24,2	28,1	524

Dinner

Beet Burger

Burgers are an excellent all-vegetable main course and can be eaten accompanied by grilled, steamed or pan-fried vegetables. Lentils are legumes rich in protein and have a good supply of iron, ideal for those suffering from anemia. The breadcrumbs in this case are made from rice cakes as they are gluten-free. Cashews are rich in plant protein and omega 6, they contain acetic acid which controls sugar absorption making this food suitable for diabetics. Beet is good for its circulatory, gut-friendly properties and is rich in folic acid; it is not recommended for those with kidney stones because it contains many oxalates.

Serve: 4

Ingredients:

- 400 g cooked lentils
- beets
- 2 tbsp whole-wheat breadcrumbs
- 1 clove of garlic
- 4-5 cashews
- ½ lemon juice
- chopped parsley to taste
- 1 tsp coconut oil
- pepper to taste

Preparation:

Boil the peeled and cut beets. (To avoid this step, you can buy pre-cooked vacuum-packed beets.)

Blend the lentils and beets in a food processor and add the bread crumbs, cashews, and garlic. (If the mixture does not seem firm enough, add more bread crumbs.)

Add pepper, coconut oil, a sprinkling of chopped parsley and lemon juice.

Let the mixture rest in the refrigerator for about 30 minutes, covered with a cloth or a layer of plastic wrap.

Form about 5 burgers, helping yourself with your hands or a hamburger mold.

Heat a nonstick skillet with a coconut oil and cook for a few minutes on each side.

Serve preferably hot.

Tips:

I love eating burgers in a fresh bun, with vegan mayonnaise, salad and a side of baked potatoes.

Great served with a mustard sauce and toasted pine nuts.

Nutrition	Carbohydrates (g)	Protein (g)	Lipids (g)	Energy (Kcal)
	24	14,9	23,1	498

TUESDAY

Breakfast

Oatmeal Porridge with Mango and Raspberry Mousse

Serve: 1

Ingredients:

- 30 g raspberries

For the mousse

- ½ mango
- 1 tbsp maple syrup

For the porridge

- 85 g oatmeal
- 175 ml almond milk
- coconut slices

Preparation:

To prepare the mousse you need to blend the mango with the maple syrup.

To prepare the porridge you need to add all the ingredients in a saucepan and cook for 5 minutes that is until the almond milk is absorbed.

Pour the porridge into a bowl and garnish with the mousse, a few raspberries and coconut slices.

Notes:

Oats are an excellent cereal that is low in gluten, rich in fiber and low on the glycemic index and therefore very suitable for people who practice sport or diabetics. Mango is a fruit with remarkable diuretic and laxative properties, an excellent source of vitamin A, potassium and calcium.

Nutrition	Carbohydrates (g)	Protein (g)	Lipids (g)	Energy (Kcal)
	24.5	11,9	4,2	181

Lunch

Curry Rice with Cashews

Serve: 4

Ingredients:

- 250 g brown rice
- 100 g soybean sprouts
- 125 g chopped peanuts
- 1 red bell pepper
- carrots
- 1 celery stalk
- garlic and onion to taste
- 2 tsp coconut oil
- a pinch of curry and ginger

Preparation:

Sauté the onion and garlic in a saucepan, then add diced carrots, bell pepper, celery and a pinch of ginger. Cook the vegetables for a few minutes to leave them crispy.

Separately cook the brown rice for as long as needed.

Serve the rice with the vegetables, then add the soybean sprouts, chopped peanuts and a pinch of curry.

Notes:

Brown rice is an excellent source of fiber, ideal for those who are gluten intolerant. It has a good amount of vitamin B, magnesium and potassium. Bell peppers, are a good source of vitamin C. Soybean sprouts are rich in vitamin C and lecithin, a substance that helps regulate cholesterol.

Nutrition	Carbohydrates (g)	Protein (g)	Lipids (g)	Energy (Kcal)
	51,6	19,1	4,5	365

Dinner

Sandwich with Mushrooms and Tempeh

Serve: 1

Ingredients:

- slices of rye bread or whole wheat bread
- 10 mushrooms
- 2-3 slices of tempeh
- half an avocado
- 1 handful of spinach
- 1 tspcoconut oil
- 1 tbsp lemon juice
- a pinch of pepper

Preparation:

Slice the mushrooms after washing them well under running water, meanwhile blanch the tempeh and heat the bread slices in a toaster.

Stuff the bread with a few slices of avocado, mushrooms, tempeh and spinach. Add the coconut oil, pepper and lemon to taste.

Notes:

Mushrooms are excellent anti-cancer agents and should be eaten once a week. Tempeh is a naturally fermented food derived from soybeans, its an excellent source of plant protein and calcium.

Nutrition	Carbohydrates (g)	Protein (g)	Lipids (g)	Energy (Kcal)
	42	11,2	6,5	506

WEDNESDAY

Breakfast

Basmati Rice, Apple and Cinnamon Pudding

Basmati rice is well suited for many preparations; rich in vitamins and minerals, it is also ideal for those who do not tolerate gluten. Apple is a superb fruit with astringent and healing properties, great for those with gastrointestinal problems. Raisins provide ready-to-use simple sugars, excellent for those who exercise. Cinnamon is an excellent muscle soother, fights nausea and relieves flu problems such as sore throats and colds.

Serve: 2

Ingredients:

- 240 ml vegetable milk
- 180 g whole-wheat basmati rice, cooked
- 40 ml maple syrup
- 1 apple
- 40 g raisins
- 40 g fresh coconut
- 1 tsp coconut oil, melted
- a pinch of cinnamon

Preparation:

Peel and dice the apple, then place it in a saucepan along with the maple syrup, cinnamon, and coconut oil and cook over medium heat while stirring.

Incorporate the milk and pre-cooked rice, stir and bring to a simmer, then lower the heat and cook for another 15 minutes or until the apple has become soft.

Transfer to the plates and add fresh shredded coconut and raisins to taste.

Let stand in the refrigerator for about 30 minutes and serve.

Tips:

Add chocolate chips or seasonal fruit of your choice.

Nutrition	Carbohydrates (g)	Protein (g)	Lipids (g)	Energy (Kcal)
	56	10,2	2,4	251

Lunch

Venus rice salad

Black rice is an excellent alternative to classic polished rice because it preserves all its nutritional properties and is very fragrant. It is used a lot in summer to make rice salads that can be enjoyed away from home. Cashews are a source of plant protein, omega 6, calcium and iron; we can use them as a snack or, as in this dish, to accompany cereals. Mango is particularly rich in vitamin A and is excellent against constipation.

Serve: 4

Ingredients:

- 200 g venus rice
- 1 carrot
- ½ lemon
- 1 mango
- ½ red onion
- 70 g Cashews
- fresh coriander and mint to taste
- 1 tsp coconut oil

Preparation:

Rinse the rice in cold water so that some of the starch it contains is washed away.

Boil salted water in a pot and pour in the rice, boil until fully cooked.

Cut the carrot into round slices.

Peel the mango and cut it into cubes.

Peel the onion and chop it.

Coarsely chop the cashews.

When the rice is cooked, drain it and run it under cold running water.

Transfer the rice to a bowl and add the previously chopped ingredients.

Chop some mint and cilantro leaves and add them to the rice.

Season with coconut oil, the lemon juice and mix everything together.

Allow to rest in the refrigerator for about half an hour.

Serve cold.

Tips:

You can add green apples or your favorite vegetables to the rice.

You can also store it in the refrigerator for a couple of days.

Nutrition	Carbohydrates (g)	Protein (g)	Lipids (g)	Energy (Kcal)
	106	26.8	46.4	954

Dinner

Vegetable sausages with peppers and potatoes

Fennel seeds have excellent digestive, anti-inflammatory and anticancer properties, as well as great flavor.

Seve: 1

Ingredients:

- 200 g smoked tofu
- 70 g cooked lentils
- 1 tbsp tomato concentrate
- 75 g cornstarch
- 20 g mustard
- 1 clove garlic
- chili pepper
- fennel seeds
- spices to taste

Preparation:

To make the sausages all you need is a blender in which you put all the ingredients and blend. I only added chopped fennel seeds for flavoring but you can put what you have or like. The important thing is that you give it a nice boost of flavor.

Take the blended dough out of the blender and with your hands make 5 equal parts to which you will give the classic shape.

Wrap them individually in baking paper and boil them in boiling water for 20 minutes.

Once cooked you can freeze them or cook them. This is how I prepare them with peppers and potatoes: peel the potatoes and cut them into chunks about an inch thick. Wash the peppers, remove the stem and seeds and cut them into strips. Put both in a pan with a drizzle of oil and if you like some thinly sliced onion. Season with salt and pepper, add a dash of water and bring to a simmer.

Finally, add the sausages cut into round slices and let them season for a few minutes. Serve the whole thing hot.

Tip: Try enjoying them grilled inside a sandwich with a little ketchup and mustard sauce.

Nutrition	Carbohydrates (g)	Protein (g)	Lipids(g)	Energy (Kcal)
	18	23,9	9,8	509

THURSDAY

Breakfast

Dessert with chia seeds and peaches

Serve: 1

Ingredients:

- 200 g coconut yogurt
- 100 g peach
- 1 tbsp chia seeds

Preparation:

Add the chia seeds and the peach to the coconut yogurt and enjoy.

Coconut yogurt is a great alternative to soy yogurt; it contains lauric acid, which is a great ally for the gut. Peach is rich in water, vitamins, minerals and it has a low glycemic index therefore it is also suitable for diabetics. Chia seeds, an excellent alternative to flax seeds, used to provide the right amount of omega 3.

Nutrition	Carbohydrates (g)	Protein (g)	Lipids (g)	Energy (Kcal)
	9.1	11,5	15	142

Lunch

Millet with Chickpeas and Eggplant

Serve: 1

Ingredients:

- 100 g of millet
- 80 g chickpeas
- 1 small eggplant
- 1 tomato for sauce
- ½ onion
- 1 tbsp coconut oil

Preparation:

Sauté shallot in coconut oil, add diced tomato and eggplant and let cook for as long as needed. When cooked, add a few basil leaves.

Separately cook millet until absorbed, calculating according to package directions the correct amount of water to add.

In another pot cook the chickpeas previously left to soak.

Then combine the millet with the eggplant sauce and chickpeas.

Notes:

Millet is a gluten-free grain with excellent digestive properties, rich in magnesium and vitamin B. Chickpeas, contain calcium, zinc and vitamins such as C, K and those of the B group. Eggplants have good diuretic abilities, excellent source of antioxidants. They also promote intestinal transit.

Nutrition	Carbohydrates (g)	Protein (g)	Lipids (g)	Energy (Kcal)
	51	20,4	8,6	360

Dinner

Zucchini and rice burger

Serves: 4

Ingredients:

- 300 g zucchini
- 250 g cooked brown rice
- 60 g of oatmeal
- 40 g of chopped walnuts
- 10 g of flaxseed flour
- 1 red onion
- 1 clove of garlic
- 15 g of fresh basil
- 10 g of fresh parsley
- 1 tsp coconut oil
- a pinch of pepper

Preparation:

In a skillet, heat a drizzle of oil and "sauté" the chopped onion and garlic until golden brown, then incorporate the sliced zucchini, salt to taste and cook for about 10 minutes or until the zucchini has softened.

In a kitchen blender, place the zucchini with onion and garlic, drained of excess cooking liquid, rice, 45 g of Oatmeal, walnuts, flaxseed flour, basil, parsley, pepper to taste, and blend until moist and fairly smooth. Transfer the dough to a bowl and incorporate the remaining 45 g of oatmeal so that the mixture is easy to work with your hands and let it rest in the refrigerator for 30 minutes, covered with plastic wrap. (If the dough is still too soft, incorporate more Oatmeal).

At this point, form 4 burgers with your hands and cook them in a preheated skillet with a drizzle of oil for about 5 minutes per side and then serve.

Notes:

You can also bake the burgers in the oven if you prefer.

Serve them with sandwiches, along with lettuce and tomatoes, or as a main dish with a side of seasonal vegetables.

Nutrition	Carbohydrates (g)	Protein (g)	Lipids (g)	Energy (Kcal)
	56	15,4	3,6	495

FRIDAY

Breakfast

Raw Brownies

Cocoa, which contains excellent antioxidants, is rich in serotonin, which can improve your mood. Nuts give you energy, almonds are rich in calcium and cashews in magnesium. Chia seeds, are an excellent alternative to flax seeds, and are useful in providing the right amount of omega-3.

Ingredients for about 6 pieces:
- 50 g almonds
- 50 g cashews
- 30 g hazelnuts
- 250 g dates
- 50 g bitter cocoa powder
- 50 g coconut flour
- 1 tbsp chia seeds
- almonds to garnish

Preparation:

Place all the ingredients in a kitchen blender (almonds, cashews, hazelnuts, dates, cocoa, coconut, Chia seeds and salt) and blend until moist and moldable.

Transfer the mixture to a baking sheet covered with baking paper and shape it with your hands so the surface becomes smooth and even.

Garnish with almonds.

Let stand in the freezer for 20 minutes.

Serve.

Tips:

If you have of time, let them rest in the refrigerator for a couple of hours (instead of in the freezer for 20 minutes)

You can store them in the refrigerator for a few days.

	Carbohydrates (g)	Protein (g)	Lipids (g)	Energy (Kcal)
Cocoa	58	20	15,2	228

Lunch

Millet with beans and green bell peppers

Serve: 1

Ingredients:

- 100 g millet
- 80 g beans
- 1 green bell pepper
- ½ onion
- 1 tsp coconut oil

Preparation:

Sauté onion in coconut oil, add diced peppers and let cook for as long as needed.

Separately cook millet until absorbed, calculating according to package directions the correct amount of water to add.

In another pot cook the beans previously left to soak.

Then combine the millet with the beans and green bell pepper.

Note:

Millet is a gluten-free grain with excellent digestive properties, rich in magnesium and B vitamins.

Nutrition	Carbohydrates (g)	Protein (g)	Lipids (g)	Energy (Kcal)
	61	16	3.4	402

Dinner

Pea frittata with sun-dried tomatoes

Serve: 1

Ingredients:

- 100 g pea flour
- 150 ml water
- chopped sun-dried tomatoes
- ½ onion
- fresh basil leaves
- a pinch of pepper

Preparation:

Fry the onion in olive oil, add the previously prepared mixture by combining the water with the flour and sun-dried tomatoes, mix well with a whisk. Add basil, sal and pepper. Cook for about 10 minutes on both sides.

Notes:

Pea flour is an excellent alternative to chickpea flour for making omelets, rich in protein, vitamins and minerals. Dried tomatoes provide flavor and are rich in lycopene, an anticancer agent that works on the prostate.

Nutrition	Carbohydrates (g)	Protein (g)	Lipids (g)	Energy (Kcal)
	46	15,6	2,8	398

SATURDAY

Breakfast

Energy Balls

Dates are excellent natural sweeteners with high energy power, therefore they are excellent for those who practice sports activities. Almonds, rich in calcium, ensure the well-being of muscles and bones. Chia seeds, an excellent alternative to flax seeds, used to provide the right amount of omega 3.

Ingredients for about 20 balls:

- 200 g pitted dates
- 100 g coconut flour
- 150 g ground almonds
- 1 tbsp chia seeds
- 1 tbsp peanut butter
- 2 tbsp coconut oil
- 1 tbsp cocoa powder

Preparation:

Place all the ingredients in a blender, and blend the mixture

Place the mixture in a bowl and knead the ingredients by hand, it will be ready when it is smooth

Let the dough rest in the refrigerator for about 1 hour

Form into balls and enjoy them

Tips:

You can store them in a container with a lid in the refrigerator for about a week.

Nutrition	Carbohydrates (g)	Protein (g)	Lipids (g)	Energy (Kcal)
	51	16,1	4,5	498

Lunch

Whole wheat pasta with pesto

Serve: 1

Ingredients:

- 100 g whole wheat pasta

For pesto

- 30 g cashews or walnuts
- 100 g basil
- 70 g yeast
- 1 tbsp coconut oil
- a pinch of pepper

Preparation:

Add the basil leaves, cashews, baking powder, salt and gradually the olive oil to the blender starting to blend at low speed, when the basil is evenly blended with the rest of the ingredients you can increase the speed of the blender until smooth.

Add the pesto to the cooked pasta and serve.

Basil is an aromatic herb rich in iron and antioxidants. Cashews known for their protein and essential fatty acid levels, in addition to their calcium and magnesium content.

Nutrition	Carbohydrates (g)	Protein (g)	Lipids (g)	Energy (Kcal)
	68	12,9	4,6	398

Dinner

Chickpea burger

Chickpeas contain a good amount of plant protein, iron and vitamin B. Brazil nuts are rich in vitamin E and selenium both with antioxidant properties. Peppers are a source of vitamin C.

Serve: 4

Ingredients:

- 200g cooked chickpeas
- 1 red onion, chopped
- 1 bell pepper cut into small pieces
- 50 g chopped brazil nuts
- 1 chopped carrot
- whole-wheat breadcrumbs to taste
- a pinch of pepper
- 1 tbsp coconut oil

Preparation:

Put all the ingredients in a blender and then add as much wholemeal breadcrumbs as will be needed to thicken it.

Blender until you get a grainy mass.

With the obtained mixture you can form about 8 burgers that you will then go and cook in a pan with a little oil for about 3-4 min. per side.

I serve the burgers with a drizzle of oil, tomato and avocado sauce, but you can unleash your creativity by adding or subtracting ingredients as you like.

Nutrition	Carbohydrates (g)	Protein (g)	Lipids (g)	Energy (Kcal)
	56	15,1	3,9	401

SUNDAY

Breakfast

Crepes with blueberry cream and spirulina

Oatmeal is good for baking because it has a low glycemic index and therefore does not cause the same blood sugar spikes given by refined flours; it also has a very low gluten content and a good amount of fiber. Blueberries are rich in antioxidants, which reduce capillary fragility and improve visual acuity. Spirulina is an algae with many beneficial properties as a source of essential amino acids, vitamins, minerals and powerful antioxidants such as chlorophylls. Coconut milk is rich in minerals such as potassium useful for physical recovery and is an excellent natural remedy for gastritis.

Serve: 4

Ingredients:

For the Crepes:

- 250 ml sparkling water
- 200 g oat flour
- 60 g potato starch
- 1 tsp maple syrup
- 1 tsp coconut oil

For the Filling:

- 1 can coconut milk
- 1 tsp maple syrup
- 5-6 blueberries
- ½ tsp spirulina powder

Preparation:

In a bowl, place the oat flour, potato starch and maple syrup: then start incorporating the water and coconut oil, stirring with a whisk and avoiding lumps, until the mixture is thick and smooth. (Caution: if it turns out too liquid, incorporate more flour and if not, more water.)

Heat a nonstick frying pan and with the help of a ladle pour in the mixture, just enough to evenly coat the base of the pan with a thin layer. (Warning: if you prefer, you can grease the pan with a little coconut oil to prevent sticking.)

Cook for about 2 minutes over medium-low heat or until the bottom surface has browned, then with the help of a spatula turn the crepe over and cook it for another 2 minutes and repeat the process until you run out of dough and get 4 crepes.

In a kitchen blender, place the solid and creamy part of the can of coconut milk, add the maple syrup, blueberries and spirulina and then blend until thick and homogenous.

Let the cream rest in the freezer for about 5 to 10 minutes or store it in the refrigerator, if you don't use it immediately, so that it becomes firmer.

Stuff the crepes with the cream and serve.

Tips:

Decorate with blueberries or dark chocolate frosting.

Nutrition	Carbohydrates (g)	Protein (g)	Lipids (g)	Energy (Kcal)
	56	14,5	3,9	401

Lunch

Rice with Lentils and Vegetables

Serve: 1

Ingredients:

- 100 g brown rice
- 80 g of lentils
- 1 carrot
- 1 zucchini
- 40 g soybean sprouts
- ½ onion
- a pinch of pepper

Preparation:

Sauté onion in coconut oil, add diced vegetables and pepper. Cook for as long as needed, leaving them slightly crispy. In another pot cook the lentils previously left to soak. Separately cook the rice for about 15 minutes, then add the lentils and vegetables and finish cooking. If desired, herbs can be added to give fragrance to the dish.

Nutrition	Carbohydrates (g)	Protein (g)	Lipids (g)	Energy (Kcal)
	68	14	3,6	398

Dinner

Millet and Lentil Meatballs

Serve: 2

Ingredients:

- 80 g millet
- 100 g red lentils, previously cooked
- 100 ml water
- 1 onion
- cloves of garlic
- 20 g oats
- 15 g chopped parsley
- 15 ml tomato concentrate
- 20 g cornmeal
- 1 pinch of pepper
- 1 tsp coconut oil

Preparation:

Peel and coarsely chop the onion and garlic.

In a kitchen blender, chop the oats until they become flour and set aside.

In a pot, boil salted water and cook the millet.

When the millet is ready, transfer it to a kitchen blender, add the lentils, onion, garlic, parsley, tomato paste and pepper to taste.

Blend, until smooth.

Transfer the mixture to a bowl and combine with the oats, stirring with a wooden spoon until smooth, slightly sticky, and moldable with your hands. (Caution: if it is still too wet, add more oats, and if not, incorporate water.)

Cover the bowl with foil and let it rest in the refrigerator for at least an hour.

After the required time has passed, take the dough back and form about 15 balls with your hands. (Note: the number will vary depending on the size).

Place the cornmeal on a plate or clean surface.

Roll each ball in the cornmeal so that it covers the entire surface.

In a skillet, heat a little oil and cook the patties for about 5 minutes or until the surface becomes brown. If you prefer bake them in the oven.

Let cool slightly and serve.

Nutrition	Carbohydrates (g)	Protein (g)	Lipids (g)	Energy (Kcal)
	65	14	4,1	428

CHAPTER 6

Why is This Dietary Regime Still so Uncommon?

"If it is so healthy, why doesn't my doctor recommend it?"

" Why doesn't my child eat many vegetables in school canteens?"

There are many reasons:

1.   *Doctors receive very limited training in nutrition.* In medical schools very few hours are dedicated to teaching this subject. They are taught more about how to treat with drugs than how to prevent (and cure) with nutrition. And this, although it is sad to admit, is mostly because of the lobbies of big pharmaceutical companies.

2.   *Politicians are pressured by powerful lobbies* (pharmaceutical, meat, egg, dairy...) to keep the demand and the consumption of all these foods high.

3.   *Some foods, such as sugars, fats and dairy products, create a real physical and psychological dependence,* just like some drugs. This happens because the gut microbiota, accustomed to animal and industrial food, makes us crave the "wrong" things. Fortunately, this also functions in reverse, once we get used to healthy food.

Our sense of taste has to get used to it. Healthy food may seem bland at first, but once we change our habits we can develop a different sensitivity and fully enjoy even the immense bouquet of a simple carrot.

It is really difficult to stop suffering from this addiction, and the only way to get rid of it is to make choosing healthy food a habit, even gradually.

4.   *Food is strongly anchored in culture, traditions, and beliefs of our families and friends.* In addition to habit, we also experience social pressure. If you change your habits, people may start to criticize you and not accept your change.

CONCLUSION

Maintaining a diet over time and making it sustainable seems to be much harder than starting a diet. While most people adhere to a diet for a short period of time, that is, until they reach their goals, what everyone finds extremely difficult is to turn the diet into a new eating regime that they can integrate into their lifestyle.

One way to induce us to eat healthy meals is a strategy known as "crowding out." It is very simple: instead of eliminating negative elements from the diet, healthier foods can be included in the diet. For example:

- you could start the meal with a certain amount of raw vegetables: this will increase satiety and alkalize the meal more;
- you can gradually incorporate new healthy eating habits: the more often you eat healthy meals, the more likely you are to get used to them and eventually start preferring them to harmful ones. It only takes a couple of weeks to turn a new habit into a habit;
- it is better to go shopping when you are not hungry: buying food when you are not full leads us to make impulse purchases and therefore not very rational purchases;
- remember that making a choice of vegetable food means making an ethical and eco-sustainable choice.

Whether our health conditions are good or whether we already have pathologies, starting a plant-based diet can bring great benefits.

We must remember that our bodies are gifted with a great ability: the ability of self-healing.

Numerous scientific studies have led to the belief that a proper diet can prevent many diseases and in many cases be curative to their total remission.

However, many people are not ready to put a healthy lifestyle at the heart of their daily lives. Often those who suffer from chronic diseases are those who usually eat foods that inflame their bodies, do not devote quality time to exercise, and live in a state of constant stress without being able to clear their negative thoughts with just a few minutes a day of meditation or deep relaxation.

I would like to cover all these topics in more detail in another forthcoming book.

For now, I am happy to share with you the knowledge I have gained about clean, green, anti-inflammatory and healing nutrition.

I sincerely hope that I have succeeded in making you more aware of how much we can increase the quality of our lives simply by "eating" not only what is readily available, but also what we have consciously and carefully chosen.

Enjoy your personal journey towards an increasingly " conscious" diet!

RECIPES

SAME TIPS BEFORE YOU START

Foods that replace salt:

Miso. A made-in-Japan condiment that is made by fermenting nutritional yeast menting soybeans or rice and barley.

Nutritional yeast Adored by vegans and made from brewer's yeast, in flakes or powder.

Seaweed. Although care should be taken not to abuse them because of their high iodine content. Dulse, wakame, spirulina, kombu, are just some of the best-known food algae, sources of minerals, calcium, iron, protein, and iodine.

Spices. Turmeric, ginger, curry, pepper, saffron, paprika will not only add flavor to the dish but act as real natural medicines, rich as they are in healing, pain-relieving and antibacterial properties.

Foods that replace oil:

Soy sauce. Not suitable for those with hypertension.

Orange juice

Grapefruit juice

Lemon juice

Apple vinegar

White wine vinegar

Coconut oil

Foods that replace sugar:

Maple and agave syrup

Stevia

Malt

Fruit juice and fruit puree

Vanilla powder

The following recipes are a selection of dishes easy to prepare demonstrating that healthy food can be good and also be very tasty.

Nutritional values refer to an average serving size of 200 grams.

And now................ Bon appetite!

SWEET AND SAVORY BREAKFASTS

Chocolate Pancakes

Time required for preparation: 10 minutes

Cooking time: 15 minutes

Serving: 2

Ingredients:

5 cups all purpose flour

½ cup cocoa powder

1 tbsp maple syrup

3 tbsp baking powder

a pinch of pepper

5 cups soy milk

1 tsp vanilla extract

1 cup water

1/2 cup melted coconut oil

1 tbsp non-dairy chocolate chips, for serving

Instructions:

In a bowl, whisk together the flour, cocoa powder, baking powder, maple syrup and pepper.

Then, after adding the soy milk, water, oil and vanilla mix with a large spoon until everything is combined,

Heat a greased pan with olive oil over medium-high heat. Drop about 1/3 cup of batter into the center of the pan. Cook until bubbles form and then flip and cook 1-2 minutes on the other side.

Tips:

Serve with chocolate chips.

Nutrition:

Calories 418

protein 11.7g

carbohydrates 59.2g

fat 17.2g

Salty Protein Pancakes

Time required for preparation: 10 minutes

Cooking time: 15 minutes

Serving: 4

Ingredients:

250 g chickpea flour

350 ml warm water

1 courgette

1 bell pepper

1 onion

1 tbsp coconut oil

aromatic herbs of your choice to taste

pepper to taste

Instructions:

In a bowl, place the chickpea flour and pepper to taste; drizzle in the water and oil and start mixing until a thick, smooth, homogeneous batter forms. Incorporate the chopped onion, zucchini and bell pepper cut into thin strips, chosen herbs, and more salt if needed, then mix well to evenly distribute the ingredients. (If the batter is too runny, incorporate more flour and if not, more water.)

At this point you can cook the pancakes, frying them in hot oil for 3-4 minutes, helping yourself with the help of a spoon to place the batter in the pan. You can also bake them in a preheated oven at 180° for about 15 minutes or until golden brown, using a spoon to place the batter on a baking sheet covered with parchment paper. Serve warm.

Notes:

You can use your favorite seasonal vegetables.

Nutrition

Calories in a serving: 298

Fat: 7.2 g

Carbohydrates: 12.5 g

Protein:12,1 g

Apple Oatmeal Muffins

Time required for preparation: 10 minutes

Cooking time: 20 minutes

Serving: 4

Ingredients:
1 apple, peeled and chopped into cubes

1 tsp cinnamon

1 tbsp maple syrup

For the batter:
¼ cup whole wheat flour

1 cup oat flour

½ cup rolled oats

1 tbsp maple syrup

A pinch of pepper

2 tsps baking powder

½ tsp baking soda

½ cup unsweetened applesauce

⅓ cup refined coconut oil, melted

⅓ cup apple cider

Instructions:

Preheat oven to 190 degrees.

Line muffin cups with muffin liners.

In a saucepan, sauté the apples over medium heat for 4 minutes. Add the maple syrup and cinnamon. When apples are soft remove from heat and set aside.

Mix the oats, flour, maple syrup, pepper, baking powder and baking soda in a bowl. Then add the applesauce, vegetable oil and cider.

Stir and add the chopped apple.

Fill muffin cups ¾ full.

Bake for about 16 minutes in the preheated oven, or until a toothpick comes out clean.

Nutrition

Calories in a serving: 256

Fat: 5.2 g

Carbohydrates: 14.5 g

Protein:12,1 g

Vanilla Pancakes

Time required for preparation: 10 minutes

Cooking time: 15 minutes

Serving: 4

Ingredients:

1 ¼ cups all-purpose flour

2 tsp baking powder

2 tbsp maple syrup

1 ¼ cups water

1 tbsp coconut oil

a pinch of pepper

Preparation:

In a large bowl sift the flour, baking powder the maple syrup and pepper form a well in the center.

In a bowl whisk together the water and coconut oil, then pour everything into the flour mixture. Stir just until everything is blended.

Heat an oiled griddle over medium-high heat.

Drop the batter by large spoonfuls onto the griddle. Cook until bubbles form in the center; then flip, then cook for 1 to 2 minutes more. Repeat with remaining batter.

Nutrition:

Calories: 264

Protein 5.4 g

Carbohydrates 48.9 g

Fat 5.1 g

One Minute Chocolate Mug Cake

Time required for preparation: 5 minutes

Cooking time: 1 minutes

Serving: 1

Ingredients:

1 tbsp cocoa powder

3 tbsps oat or spelt flour

2 tsps maple syrup

1/4 tsp baking powder

2-3 tsps coconut oil

3 tbsps almond milk

1/2 tsp vanilla extract

Instructions

Combine the dry ingredients and mix well.

Add the liquid, stir and transfer to a saucer, ramekin or coffee cup.

Bake in microwave oven for 30-40 seconds

Nutrition:

Calories: 180

Fat: 8g

Carbs: 28g

Protein: 5.5g

Avocado Toast

Time required for preparation: 2 minutes

Cooking time: 3 minutes

Serving: 2

Ingredients:

2 slices whole bread toasted

1/2 – 3/4 ripe avocado

1-2 tbsps vegan cheese

1 pinch red pepper flake

1 pinch sesame seeds

1 tbsp coconut oil

Instructions

Toast bread in the oven or toaster.

Top with ripe avocado and use a fork to smash and garnish with vegan cheese, red pepper flake, sesame seeds and coconut oil.

Nutrition:

Serving: 1 two-slice servings

Calories: 293

Carbohydrates: 30.3 g

Protein: 6.2 g

Fat: 1.9 g

Simple Vegan Omelette

Ingredients:

3 cups firm silken tofu

2 tbsps hummus

2 tbsps nutritional yeast

2 cloves garlic (chopped)

a pich of pepper

1/4 tsp paprika

1 tsp coconut oil

1 tsp cornstarch or arrowroot powder

Filling:

1 heaping cup veggies of choice (onion, spinach, tomato, mushroom)

Toppings:

Fresh herbs

Instructions

Preheat the oven to 190 C.

Prepare the vegetables, drain and dry the tofu.

Heat a skillet, suitable for the oven, over medium heat. Once hot, add the olive oil and garlic and cook for 1-2 minutes.

Transfer the garlic to the food processor, along with the other omelet ingredients (tofu - cornstarch) and blend.

Add 2 tablespoons of water to fluidify and set aside.

In the still hot skillet over medium heat, cook the vegetables with a coconut oil and add pepper.

I like to start with the onions and mushrooms, then add the tomatoes and finally the spinach. Set aside.

Remove the pan from the heat and make sure it is covered with enough oil so the omelet does not stick.

Add back 1/4 of the vegetables and pour in the omelet batter, spreading it gently with a spoon. The batter should be thin and even.

Cook over medium heat on the stove for 5 minutes, until the edges begin to dry out. Then place in the oven and bake about 10 to 12 minutes.

In the last few minutes of baking, carefully add the remaining vegetables on top of the omelet and bake 1-2 more minutes to warm through.

Gently remove from the oven and gently fold in with a spatula.

Serve with desired toppings.

Nutrition

Calories: 232

Carbohydrates: 22 g

Protein: 22 g

Fat: 7.8 g

Green Smoothies

Green smoothies are composed of vegetables and fruits; they tend to be sweet, although they contain a lower level of sugar than regular smoothies. This is because they contain more vegetables than fruits.

One of the ingredients most often included in green smoothies is spinach, which makes the smoothie green and have a rather neutral flavor, does not add bitterness to the final product, and therefore can be well combined with many ingredients. These vegetables have very interesting nutritional characteristics because they have a good amount of fiber, as well as vitamins such as A, C, and K. They also have a good amount of calcium and antioxidants.

Avocado is often added to make the smoothie creamier and rich in nutrients, such as useful fats for the body and minerals such as potassium.

Frozen fruit, such as banana, is also often added to make the smoothie taste sweeter. Another ingredient used in green smoothies is coconut water, which makes them more refreshing.

To make these smoothies more proteic, add oil seeds such as chia seeds, sunflower seeds, flax seeds, etc... or your favorite dried fruits such as walnuts, almonds, nuts, etc...

Avocado, Cocoa and Coffee Smoothie

Ingredients:

250 ml coconut or almond milk.

225 ml cold espresso coffee

½ avocado in pieces

10 - 15 almonds, blanched

½ tsp maple syrup

½ cup crushed ice

½ tsp cocoa powder

1 tsp turmeric

Preparation:

Garnish with a pinch of cocoa powder on the top

Nutrition:

Calories: 264

Fat: 5, 4 g

Carbs: 8,3 g

Fiber: 3,8 g

Protein: 14.6 g

Dark Chocolate and Walnuts Smoothie

Ingredients:

150 ml almond milk

1 small banana

20 g of 80 % dark chocolate

4 walnuts

1 tbsp chia seeds

1 tbsp of cocoa

Preparation:

Garnish with a pinch of cocoa powder on the top

Nutrition:

Calories: 269

Fat: 9, 4 g

Carbs: 11,9 g

Fiber: 4,2 g

Protein: 15.6 g

Cinnamon Blueberry Smoothie

Ingredients:

1 cup unsweetened soy milk

1/2 cup blueberries

1/2 avocado

1 cup spinach or kale

2 tbsps almond butter

1/8 tsp cinnamon

Nutrition:

Calories: 224

Fat: 6,9 grams

Carbs: 10 grams

Fiber: 14 grams

Protein: 8,6 grams

Banana, Strawberries and Tofu Smoothie

Ingredients:

1 cup soy milk

140 g velvety tofu

2 cups fresh strawberries

1 banana

1 tsp maple syrup

Nutrition:

Calories: 130

Fat: 6.9 grams

Carbs: 4 grams

Fiber: 3,2 grams

Protein: 18 grams

Coconut, Mango and Avocado Smoothie

Ingredients:

½ avocado

1 heaped tsp bitter cocoa powder

120 ml coconut milk

2 small slices of fresh coconut

½ cup mango cut into pieces

10 almonds

2 ice cubes

Preparation:

Blend all the ingredients together, you can add a sprinkle of coffee powder, after pouring it into a glass.

Nutrition:

Calories: 286

Fat: 6, 4 g

Carbs: 12,9 g

Fiber: 4,8 g

Protein: 16,9 g

Papaya and Dark Chocolate Smoothie

Ingredients:

150 gr fresh papaya

25 g dark chocolate

2 ice cubes

120 ml soy milk

120 ml vegetable yogurt

1 tsp maple syrup

½ tsp turmeric

Nutrition:

Calories: 302

Fat: 9,2 g

Carbs: 11,9 g

Fiber: 4,4 g

Protein: 15.6 g

Pineapple and Spinach Smoothie

The combination of pineapple - fat burning - and spinach - remineralizing - will be a real boost for the body.

Ingredients:

2 handfuls of spinach

1 cup of water

3 slices of pineapple cut into small pieces

1 peach

1 banana

Nutrition:

Calories: 256

Fat: 5,9 g

Carbs: 9,6 g

Fiber: 1,6 g

Protein: 4,9 g

Strawberry Zucchini Chia Smoothie

Ingredients:

1 cup coconut water

1/2 cup fresh strawberries

1 cup chopped zucchini

3 tbsps chia seeds

Nutrition:

Calories: 210

Fat: 9,4 grams

Carbs: 11 grams

Fiber: 2,9 grams

Protein: 5,9 grams

Fresh Fennel Smoothie

Ingredients:

1 cup baby spinach

1 cup soy milk

1/2 lime

1/2 fennel

2 walnuts

4 almonds

2 tbsps oat flakes

a sprig of fennel

a pinch of pepper

Nutrition:

Calories: 281

Fat: 15,1 grams

Carbs: 12 grams

Fiber: 6 grams

Protein: 11 grams

Coconut Strawberry Mint Smoothie

Ingredients:

1/2 cup coconut milk

1/2 cup strawberry

2 tbsps shredded coconut

½ avocado

6 mint leaves

Nutrition:

Calories: 224

Fat: 6,5 grams

Carbs: 12 grams

Fiber: 6 grams

Protein: 5 grams

Carrot, Green Apple and Radish Smoothie

Radish is a natural detoxifier that can increase oxygen levels in the blood; it also contains enzymes that cleanse the liver. It is an important natural supplement that we should often include in smoothies.

Ingredients:

2 radishes

1 green apple

1 carrot

A few slices of fresh ginger

1 glass of water (200 ml)

Nutrition:

Calories: 101

Fat: 1,2 g

Carbs: 10,6 g

Fiber: 1,9 g

Protein: 2,9 g

WFPB DRESSING "NO BLENDER"

Quick Hummus Dressing

Ingredients:

1 cup hummus

2 tbsp lemon juice

½ tbs nutritional yeast

water to thin

Preparation:

Stir to combine all ingredients and add water until desired consistency is achieved

Tips:

To get a spicy flavor, add 2 tsp of curry powder and 1 tbsp of maple syrup

These sauces will make all your recipes tastier

Thain Dressing

Ingredients:

6 tbsp smooth tahini (sesame seed sauce)

3 tbsp lemon juice

1 ½ tbsp maple syrup

Water to thin

Preparation:

Stir to combine all ingredients and add water until desired consistency is achieved

BBQ Dressing

Ingredients:

1 cup hummus

2 tbsp lemon juice

½ tbs nutritional yeast

1 tbs maple syrup

2tsp smoked paprika powder

½ tsp garlic powder

¼ tsp black pepper

1 pinch of cayenne

Water to thin

Preparation:

Stir to combine all ingredients and add water until desired consistency is achieved

ONE-DISH MEALS

Vegan Meatballs

Time required for preparation: 10 minutes

Cooking time: 25 minutes

Servings: 4

Ingredients:

6 tbsp chopped almonds

1 cup water

6 cups drained and rinsed chickpeas,

1 cup breadcrumbs

1/2 cup nutritional yeast

a pinch of garlic and onion powder

1 tsp oregano

Instructions:

Preheat the oven to 190 degrees.

In a small bowl, mix together the ground almonds and water.

Let stand for a few minutes.

In a food processor, blend the chickpeas.

Pour the almond/water mixture, bread crumbs, garlic powder, onion powder, oregano, and salt into a bowl. Mix with a large spoon until well combined.

Form into balls (about a large spoonful each) and place them on a baking sheet lined with baking paper.

Place in the oven and bake for 30 minutes, turning once halfway through baking.

Serve the meatballs with BBQ sauce - see recipe in the dressing section.

Nutrition

- Calories in a serving: 445
- 12 g of fat
- Carbohydrates: 48,9 g
- 16 g of protein

Notes:

Nutritional yeast appears in several plant-based recipes. But you don't have to be a vegan to eat it; it has a flavor reminiscent of aged cheese, which is why it turns out to be popular among those who are lactose intolerant.
"Nutritional yeast" refers to the inactive form of common brewer's yeast, whether in flakes or powder form. It therefore has no leavening power. Its texture somewhat resembles that of potato flakes.
It can be used to season pasta dishes or in a variety of recipes such as meatballs, sauces and vegetables.
The value of nutritional yeast lies in its nutritional values. It is naturally very rich in all 9 of the essential amino acids of which protein is made up of. It contains many B group

vitamins and several minerals. Despite the strong flavor, the natural salt content is really low (0.5%).

If you are wondering where to buy it, don't worry because today nutritional yeast flakes can be easily found in larger supermarkets, all organic food stores, or, more conveniently, online.

Chickpea Brurger

Time required for preparation: 10 minutes

Cooking time: 10 minutes

Serve: 4

Ingredients:

200g cooked chickpeas

1 red onion, chopped

1 bell pepper cut into small pieces

50 g chopped almonds

1 chopped carrot

whole-wheat breadcrumbs to taste

a pinch of pepper

1 tbsp coconut oil

1 tsp nutritional yeast

Preparation:

Put all the ingredients in a blender and then add as much wholemeal breadcrumbs as will be needed to thicken it.

Blender until you get a grainy mass.

With the obtained mixture you can form about 8 burgers that you will then go and cook in a pan with a little oil for about 3-4 min. per side.

I serve the burgers with a tahini dressing - see recipe in the dressing section.

Nutrition:

Calories in a serving: 401
4,9 g of fat
Carbohydrates: 56 g
16 g of protein

Sandwich with Mushrooms, Avocado and Tempeh

Time required for preparation: 10 minutes

Cooking time: 5 minutes

Serve: 1

Ingredients:

slices of rye bread with sourdough

10 mushrooms

2-3 slices of tempeh

half an avocado

1 handful of spinach

1 tbsp coconut oil

1 tbsp lemon juice

a pinch of pepper

Preparation:

Slice the mushrooms after washing them well under running water, meanwhile blanch the tempeh and heat the bread slices in a toaster.

Stuff the bread with a few slices of avocado, mushrooms, tempeh and spinach. Add the coconut oil, pepper and lemon to taste.

Nutrition:

- Calories in a serving: 420
- 6,5 g of fat
- Carbohydrates: 42 g
- 14 g of protein

Avocado, tofu and asparagus tartare

Time required for preparation: 20 minutes

Cooking time: 10 minutes

Servings: 2

Ingredients:
250 g asparagus
80 g tofu cut into cubes
1 lime
4 tbsp coconut oil
a handful of toasted pine nuts
a pinch of ground mustard
a pinch of pepper and garlic powder
fresh basil

Preparation:
1. Cook the asparagus for 10 minutes.
2. Emulsify oil, garlic, juice of half a lime, basil and mustard powder.
3. Dice the avocado and drizzle the remaining lime juice over it so it doesn't darken.
4. Season chopped asparagus, avocado and tofu in a large bowl with the oil emulsion.

5. Prepare the tartare by pouring half of the compost into a ramekin previously placed in the center of the plate.
6. Garnish with toasted pine nuts.

Nutrition:

- Calories in a serving: 440
- 35 g of fat
- Carbohydrates: 5,9 g
- 18 g of protein

Pizza with Basil and Olives

Time required for preparation: 10 minutes

Cooking preparation: 30 minutes

Servings: 4

Ingredients:

For the pizza sauce

1 can diced tomatoes

1 tbsp coconut oil

1/2 cup fresh basil leaves, rinsed thoroughly

2 garlic cloves, peeled and chopped

1 tsp onion powder

1/4 tsp dried sage

¼ tsp red chili flakes

1 tbsp nutritional yeast

For the pizza base

4 pitas whole bread

200 g shredded vegan mozzarella

Rinse and thinly slice 1 cup mixed vegetables of your choice (tomatoes; eggplant; onion; green pepper; mushroom)

1/3 cup pitted olives, finely chopped

1 tablespoon extra-virgin olive oil

5 basil leaves, washed and split into tiny pieces

Intructions:

To prepare the sauce, follow these steps:

1. In a blender, blend on low speed until the basil and garlic are very tiny bits, then add the coconut oil and blend until smooth.
2. Put diced tomatoes, the onion powder and cook for about 20 minutes, or until the sauce has reduced somewhat and thickened in a saucepan.

To prepare the pizza, follow these steps:

1. Set the oven to 500 degrees Fahrenheit. Prepare a baking sheet by lining it with parchment paper and setting it aside.
2. Spread the pizza sauce over the pitas in a uniform layer. Place the vegan mozzarella on top and sprinkle the cut vegetables and olives, the basil and garlic emulsion and dried sage.
3. Bake for about 8 minutes.
4. Sprinkle the basil leaves on top of them to finish. For about three weeks, you can store leftovers in the freezer in an airtight container.

Nutrition:

- Calories in a serving: 400

- 10 g of total fat
- Carbohydrates: 64 g
- 5 g of dietary fiber
- 10 g of protein

Kamut Noodles with Pesto

Time required for preparation: 5 minutes

Cooking time: 15 minutes

Servings: 2

Ingredients:

1 bunch of freshly picked basil leaves
6 cups of well washed cooked whole kamut
noodles
1 bunch of fresh parsley
1 bunch of fresh cilantro
1 tbsp coconut oil
1 tbls nutritional yeast
a pinch of pepper

Instructions:

1. Combine the coconut oil, basil, parsley, nutritional yeast and cilantro in a blender until well combined. Blend until the mixture is smooth.
2. Combine the cooked noodles and the sauce in a large mixing basin. Toss to combine flavours.

Nutrition

- Calories in a serving: 355
- Total fat: 21
- Carbohydrates: 36 g
- Dietary fiber: 1 g
- Protein: 9 g

Quinoa Bowl

Time required for preparation: 10 minutes

Time required for cooking: 10 minutes

Servings: 4

Ingredients:

1 cup quinoa, well washed

2 cups cooked black beans

1 tsp cumin seeds,

2 minced garlic cloves,

2 limes (squeezed)

avocado thinly sliced

fresh cilantro (about one handful)

Instructions:

1. Pour the quinoa inside the boiling water and mix. Cook it for about 8 minutes.
2. While that's happening, in a small skillet combine the black beans, garlic, cumin and lime juice.
3. Simmer for 10 minutes.
4. Combine the quinoa and warmed beans in a large mixing basin until well combined. Place the avocado and cilantro over the top and serve immediately.

Nutrition:

- 420 calories per serving
- 9 g of total fat
- Carbohydrates: 70 g
- 18 g of dietary fiber
- 2 g of sugar
- 10 g of protein

Roasted vegetables

Time required for preparation: 10 minutes

Cooking time: 17 minutes

Servings: 2

Ingredients:

2 heads garlic

2 big eggplants

2 large shallots peeled, then quartered

2 carrots, peeled and cut into cubes

1 giant parsnip, peeled and cut into cubes

1 small green bell pepper

1 broccoli

1 sprig of thyme, with leaves plucked

2 tbsp coconut oil,

A pinch of pepper

Ingredients for garnishing

½ lemon divided into wedges and ½ squeezed

1 / 8 cup fennel bulb, finely chopped

Instructions:

1. Preheat the oven until the temperature reaches 425 degrees Fahrenheit.
2. Prepare a deep roasting pan by lining it with aluminum foil and gently greasing it with oil. Toss in all the vegetables, herbs and pepper to taste.
3. Add the remaining oil and lemon juice until well combined. Toss everything together well.
4. To cover the roasting pan, place a piece of aluminum foil. Place this on the center oven rack and bake for 30 minutes. Remove the aluminum foil from the pan. After cooling for a few minutes, divide evenly among plates.
5. Finish with a fennel bulb, finely chopped and a slice of lemon for garnish. Before you begin to eat, squeeze the lemon juice over the top of the meal.

Nutrition:

- Calories in a serving: 164
- Fat: 4.2 g
- Carbohydrates: 22.5 g
- 6.3 g of dietary fiber
- 9.2 g of protein

Kale Salad

Time required for preparation: 10 minutes

Cooking time: 5 minutes

Serving: 2

Ingredients:

1 avocado cut into slices
1 head of kale, washed, dried and thinly sliced
1 medium tomato sliced

For Dressings

1 tbsp coconut oil
1 tsp dijon mustard
4 drops of liquid stevia extract
1 tbsp lemon juice

Garnishes include:

A few pumpkin seeds
A few pieces of tempeh that have been seared

Instructions:

1. In a bowl, mix together all the dressing ingredients and use them to dress the kale.
2. Put in a salad bowl the avocado, the tomato and the kale.

3. Season and serve with garnishes.

Nutrition:

- Calories in a serving: 248
- Fat: 4.2 g
- Saturated fat: 2.8 g
- Carbohydrates: 13.5 g
- Fiber: 3.3 g

Italian Minestrone

Time required for preparation: 15 minutes
Cooking time: 15 minutes
Servings: 2

"Minestrone" is rich in alkaline nutrients and is also incredibly delicious. Preparing it simply means doing your body an excellent service. This vegetable soup is a good source of minerals and fiber; it also contains several vitamins and phytonutrients, which act as antioxidants.

The mix of carrots, zucchini, and sweet potatoes in this dish leaves no doubt that it is tasty, nutritious, and healthy.

Ingredients:

1 bunch of basil

1 carrot

1 zucchini

2 cups of mashed sweet potato

1 red onion

1 tbsp coconut oil

1 liter of vegetable broth

1 cup tomato juice

1/2 cup cooked beans

a pinch of pepper

1 tbsp nutritional yest

Instructions:

1. Peel and dice the onion, the carrot and the zucchini.
2. For 2 minutes, heat the coconut oil in a large pan and fry the vegetables.
4. Stir in the tomato juice, stock, and beans until well combined.
5. Bring the mixture to a boil, add the mashed sweet potato and decrease the heat to a low level; cook for 20 minutes.
6. Stir in the basil and add pepper and nutritional yeast.

Nutrition:

- Calories in a serving: 110
- Fat: 6.4 g
- Saturated fat: 2.8 g
- Carbohydrates: 11.3 g
- Fiber: 3.5 g

Gazpacho with Creamy Cucumber

Preparation time: 15 minutes

Serving: 2

Ingredients:
2 cucumbers
1 ripe avocado
1 key Lime,
2 handfuls of basil,
A pinch of pepper
2 cups of water
1 tbsp coconut

Instructions:
1. Peel the cucumber and remove any seeds that may be present. Cut the avocado into pieces.
2. Place all ingredients in a blender and purée until smooth. Add the pepper.
3. Put the soup to cool in the refrigerator for around 10 minutes.
4. To finish, add basil leaves, oil and thinly sliced cucumber to the dish and garnish with them.
5. Serve

Nutrition

- Calories in a serving: 135

- Fat: 2.4 g
- Saturated fat: 2.4 g
- Carbohydrates: 11.3 g
- Fiber: 3.5 g

Mango Salad

Preparation time: 15 minutes

Srving: 2

Ingredients:

6 plum tomatoes

1/2 cup mango chunks (diced)

1 tomatillo (tomatillos are a type of tomato).

1 cup red onions

1/4 cup chopped green bell peppers

½ cup cilantro leaves

a pinch of onion powder

2 tsp lime juice

1 tbsp coconut oil

Instructions:

1. Cut all the vegetables thin and put them in a salad bowl.
2. Add the mango, lime juice and seasonings
3. Enjoy your Quick Mango Salad!

Nutrition:

- Calories in a serving: 110
- Fat: 1.4 g
- Saturated fat: 1.8 g
- Carbohydrates: 15.3 g
- Fiber: 2.5 g

Chickpeas Salad

Preparation time: 10 minutes plus 30 minutes in the refrigerator

Serving: 4

Ingredients

2 cups chickpeas that have been cooked

2 tbsp vegan mayonnaise

¼ cup red onions, roughly chopped 1/2 cup of

chopped green bell peppers

1 tsp dill

a pinch of onion powder

Instructions:

1. In a large bowl, combine chickpeas and vegan mayonnaise. Mix.
2. Blend all remaining ingredients and pour them into the salad bowl with the chickpeas. Mix up.
3. Refrigerate it for 30 minutes before serving.
4. Toss the Chickpea Salad together and serve.

Nutrition:

- Calories in a serving: 110
- Fat: 5.4 g
- Carbohydrates: 11.3 g
- Fiber: 4.5 g

Sweet Potatoes Salad "

Preparation time: 10 minutes plus 30 minutes in the refrigerator

Servings: 4

Ingredients
2 sweet potatoes

2 zucchini

1 carrot

1/2 cup of almond

1 tbsp coconut oil

a pinch of pepper

a pinch of Ginger Powder

4 tbsp orange juice

•

Instructions:
1. 1 In a blender, combine the almond, coconut oil, orange Juice, ginger powder, until smooth
2. Boil carrot, sweet potatoes, zucchinis, and onion: let them cool and cut them into slices.
3. Combine everything in a salad bowl and mix.
4. Allow 30 minutes of cooling time in the refrigerator before serving.
5. Serve

Nutrition:
- Calories in a serving: 274
- Fat: 5.4 g
- Carbohydrates: 19.3 g
- Fiber: 4.5 g

Pickle Salad

Preparation time: 15 minutes

Serving: 2

Ingredients:

1 cup cucumbers, cut thinly

1/2 cup lime juice,

½ cup apple cider vinegar

1 tbsp dill

1 tsp coriander

A pinch of paprika

4 tbsp orange juice

Instructions:

1. Crush the coriander using a pestle and mortar.
2. Combine the cucumber slices, coriander, and the remaining ingredients in a jar with a tight-fitting cover. Shake it up thoroughly.
3. Allow it to infuse for 6–8 hours.
4. Serve your Pickle Salad and enjoy it.

Nutrition:

- Calories in a serving: 110

- Fat: 2.4 g
- Carbohydrates: 16.3 g
- Fiber: 3.6 g

Beans in a Baked Tomato Sauce

Preparation time: 15 minutes

Cooking time: 30 minutes

Serving: 4

Ingredients:

6 tomatoes

3 cups cooked beans

1/4 cup sliced green bell peppers

¼ cup onion, diced

1 tbsp date syrup

a pinch of paprika

Instructions:

Blend the Plum Tomatoes, Date Syrup and herbs until they have a smooth consistency in a blender.

Combine the tomato mixture, bell peppers, onions, and Garbanzo Beans in a large saucepan.

Cook, on medium heat for approximately 30 minutes, or until tender vegetables.

Serve.

Nutrition:

Calories in a serving: 110

Fat: 6.4 g

Carbohydrates: 11.3 g

Fiber: 3.5 g

Snacks

Baked Crispy Chickpeas

Time required for preparation: 10 minutes

Cooking time: 20 minutes

Serving: 2

Ingredients:

250 g cooked chickpeas

30 g whole spelt flour

1 tbsp coconut oil

a pinch of paprika

a pinch of dried rosemary

Preparation:

1   Transfer the chickpeas to a bowl and add the paprika, rosemary and mix well with a spoon. Add the flour and coconut oil and continue to mix well.

2   Transfer the chickpeas to a baking sheet with parchment paper. Bake them in the oven at 180 degrees for about 20 minutes.

They are crispy and super tasty!

Nutrition:

•   Calories in a serving: 135

•   Fat: 1,9 g

- Carbohydrates: 11,3 g
- Fiber: 6,5 g
- Protein: 6,4 g

Spicy Chocolate Breadsticks

Time required for preparation: 15 minutes

Serving: 2

Ingredients:

- 8 whole-grain breadsticks
- 150 g dark chocolate
- a pinch of chili powder

Preparation:

1   Melt the chocolate in the microwave.

2   Combine the tip of a teaspoon of chili powder with the chocolate and stir.

3   Pour the chocolate into a tall glass and let it cool a bit for 3-4 minutes.

4   Dip half of the breadsticks in the melted chocolate and let them dry for a few moments.

Nutrition:

- Calories in a serving: 230
- Fat: 6,1 g
- Carbohydrates: 23,9 g
- Fiber: 6,1 g
- Protein: 6,1 g

Dates Balls

- ## *Ingredients for about 20 balls:*
  - 200 g pitted dates
  - 100 g coconut flour
  - 150 g ground almonds
  - 1 tbsp chia seeds
  - 1 tbsp peanut butter
  - 1 tbsp coconut oil
  - 1 tbsp cocoa powder

Preparation:

Place all the ingredients in a blender, and blend the mixture

Place the mixture in a bowl and knead the ingredients by hand, it will be ready when it is smooth

Let the dough rest in the refrigerator for about 1 hour

Form into balls and enjoy them

Tips:

You can store them in a container with a lid in the refrigerator for about a week.

Nutrition:

- Calories in a serving: 329
- Fat: 6,1 g

- Carbohydrates: 45,9 g
- Fiber: 4,1 g
- Protein: 9,1 g

DESSERTS

Chocolate cream

Preparation time: 5 minutes
Serving: 2

Ingredients:

100 g agave syrup
40 g cocoa powder
5 g vanilla powder
50 g almond or soy milk
a pinch of cinnamon

Instructions:

Mix all ingredients except cinnamon vigorously.
Sprinkle cinnamon to taste.
You can add more milk and heat it up to obtain a delicious
hot drink.

Pumpkin Tiramisu

Preparation time: 30 minutes
Serving: 4

Ingredients:

4 whole wheat spelt toasts or 4 dry spelt cookies

1 cup pumpkin puree

2 tbsp agave syrup

4 tbsp of soy milk

2 cups coffee

bitter cocoa

Instructions:

Blend the pumpkin with soy milk and agave syrup
Place the rusks on the bottom of a mug a -single portion.
Pour over the cups of coffee.
Cover with the pumpkin cream and level off well.
Sprinkle with unsweetened cocoa powder.

The recipe's origins:

Tiramisu', which means adds life, is a typical Italian dessert created in the mid-1800s in the city of Trevis. It seems that this dessert was created by a mistress of a pleasure house so she could offer it to her customers. She considered this dessert to be an aphrodisiac.

Chocolate salami

Preparation time: 30 minutes
Serving: 4

Ingredients:

300 g dark chocolate min 85 %.

150 g whole wheat cookies

200 g soy milk

200 g dried fruit

1 tsp cinnamon powder

1 tsp turmeric powder

Instructions:

Chop the whole wheat cookies and the dried fruit together. Melt the chocolate in the microwave and let it cool off. Add the soy milk and the chopped whole wheat cookies and dried fruit. Mix well and pour everything on a sheet of baking paper.

Wrap the baking paper into a cylinder and roll up the ends to close it.

Chill the roll in the fridge for at least 2 hours.

Unroll and cut the chocolate salami into slices.

Deepening:

Typical Italian dessert prepared especially after the Easter holidays in order to reuse the leftover Easter egg chocolate.

Chocolate cream

Preparation time: 30 minutes
Serving: 4

Ingredients:

400 g cooked black beans

1/2 cup beloved cocoa

3 cups almond milk

1 tbsp agave syrup

1 tsp cinnamon powder

crumbled dried fruit

garnish with sliced strawberries

Preparation:

Place all ingredients in a large bowl and blend with an immersion blender

Divide the cream into 4 cups and chill them in the refrigerator for an hour.

Garnish with slices of strawberries.

Chocolate and yogurt cake

Preparation time: 20 minutes

Serving: 4

Ingredients:

1 jar of vegetable yogurt 125 g

1 jar of sunflower oil

1/2 a jar of agave syrup

1 jar of almond or soy milk

2 jars whole spelt flour

1 tbsp cocoa

1 sachet of baking powder

Preparation:

Empty the yogurt jar into a large bowl.

Add all the other ingredients except for the cocoa and mix well until you get a creamy mixture.

Divide the dough into two bowls and in one add the bitter cocoa and stir well.

Line a cake tin with baking paper and pour the dough of the first bowl in it then pour the other cacao dough in the center of the cake tin.
Bake at 180 degrees for 25 minutes.

Made in the USA
Coppell, TX
15 January 2023

11147287R00098